This Book Belongs To:

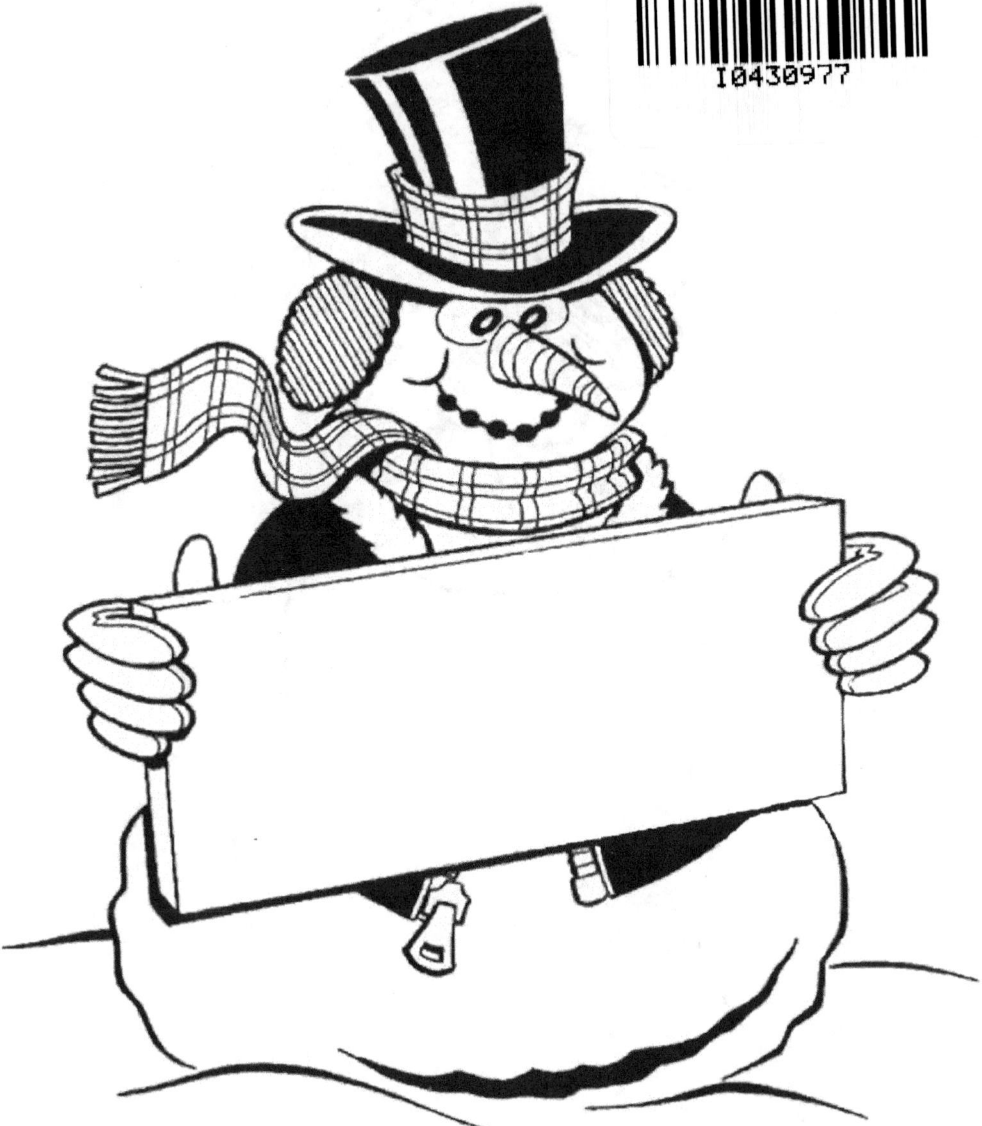

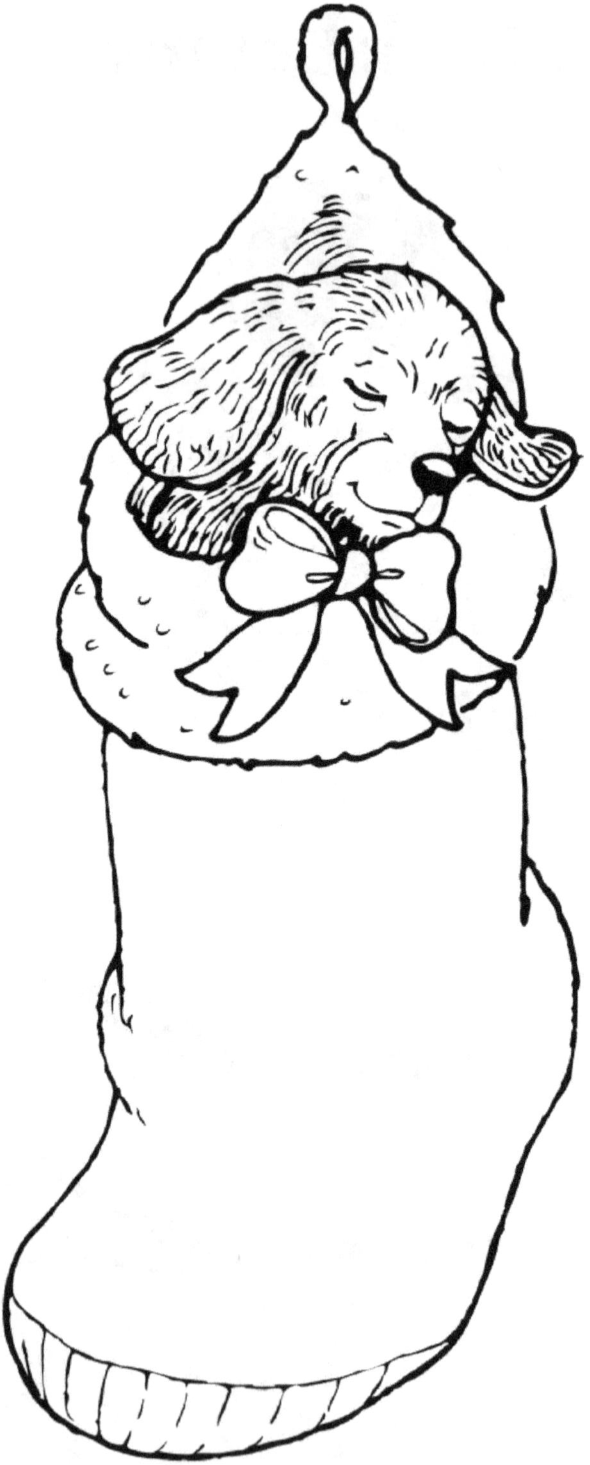

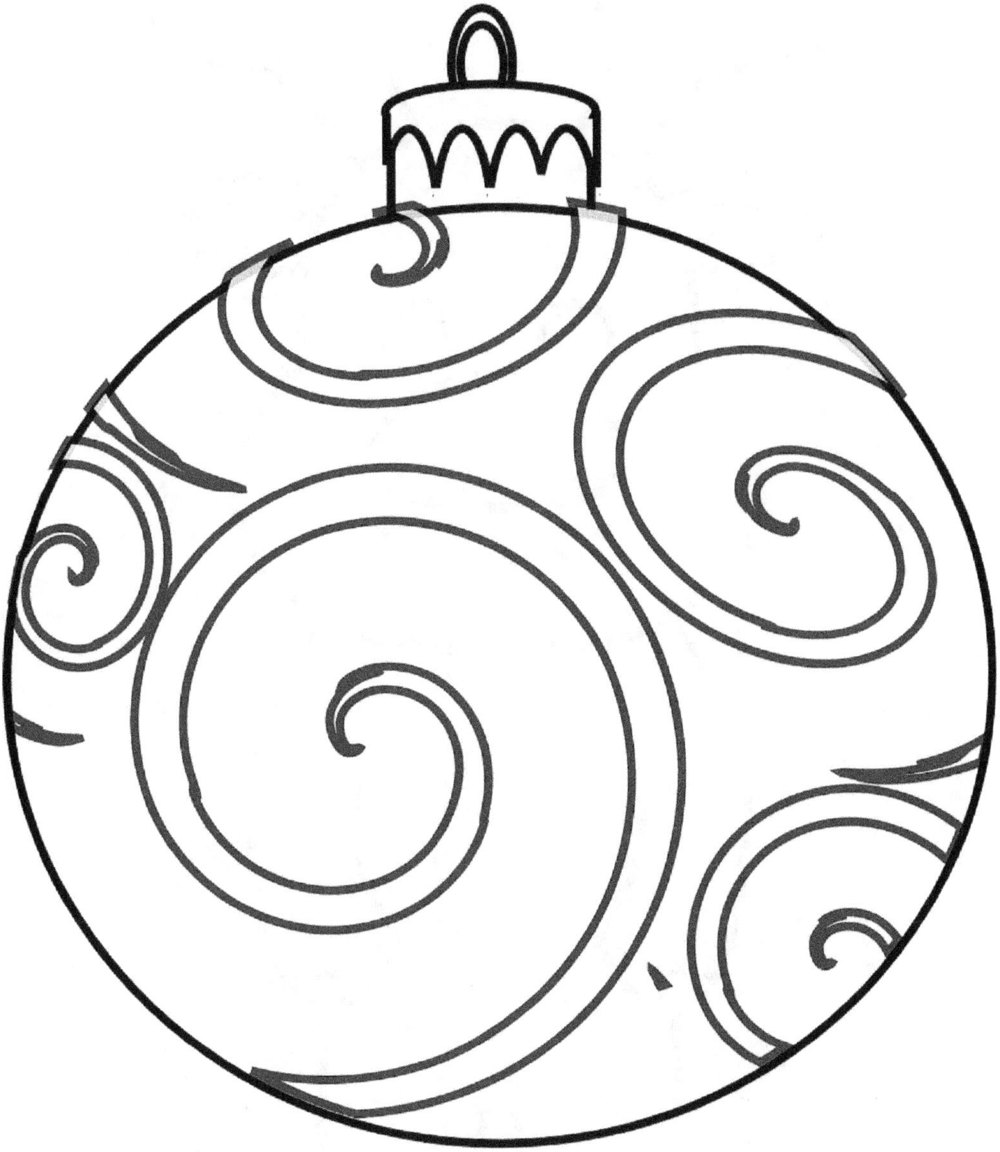

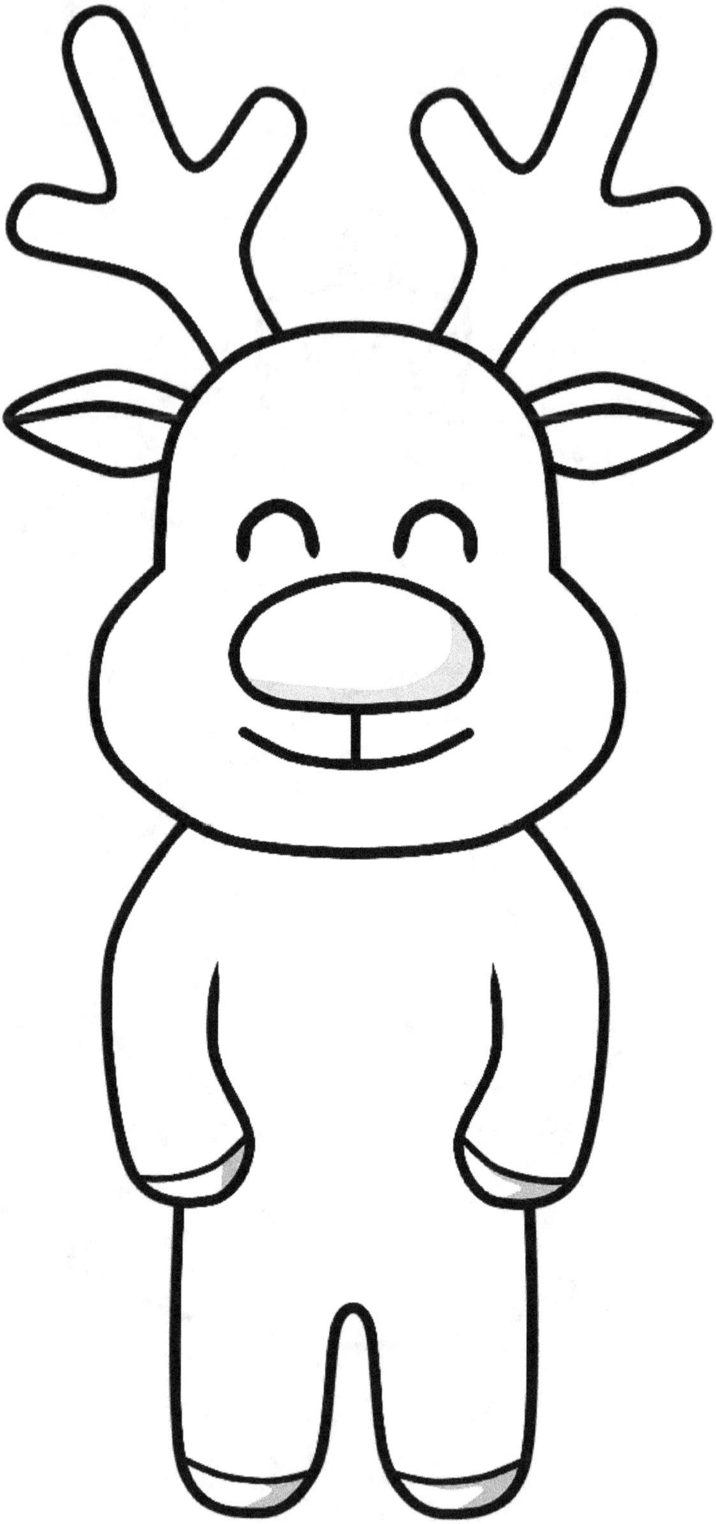

CONNECT THE DOTS

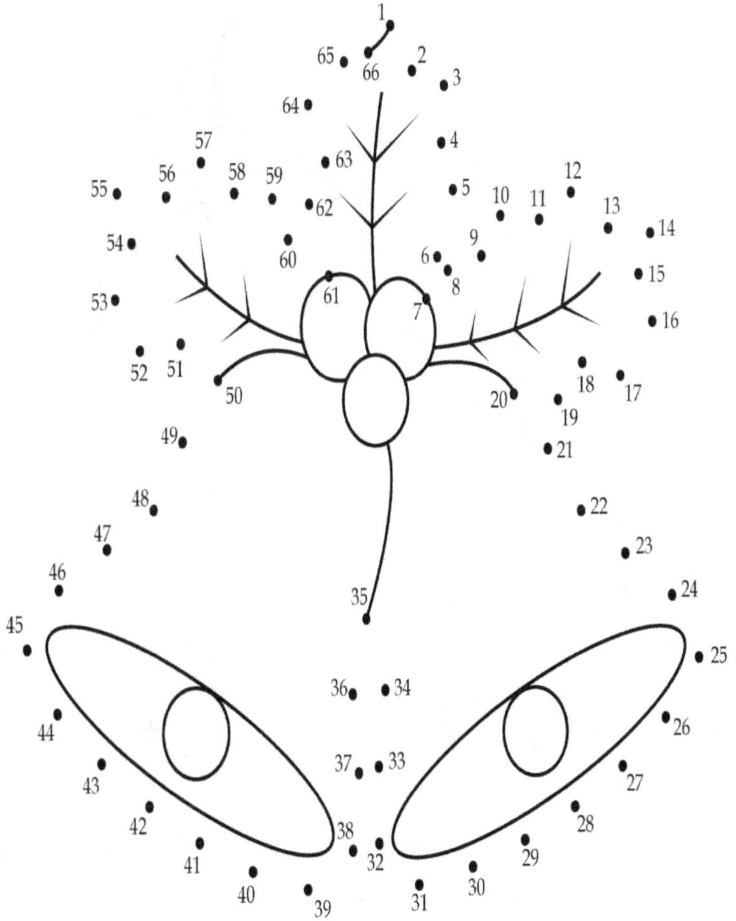

CONNECT THE DOTS

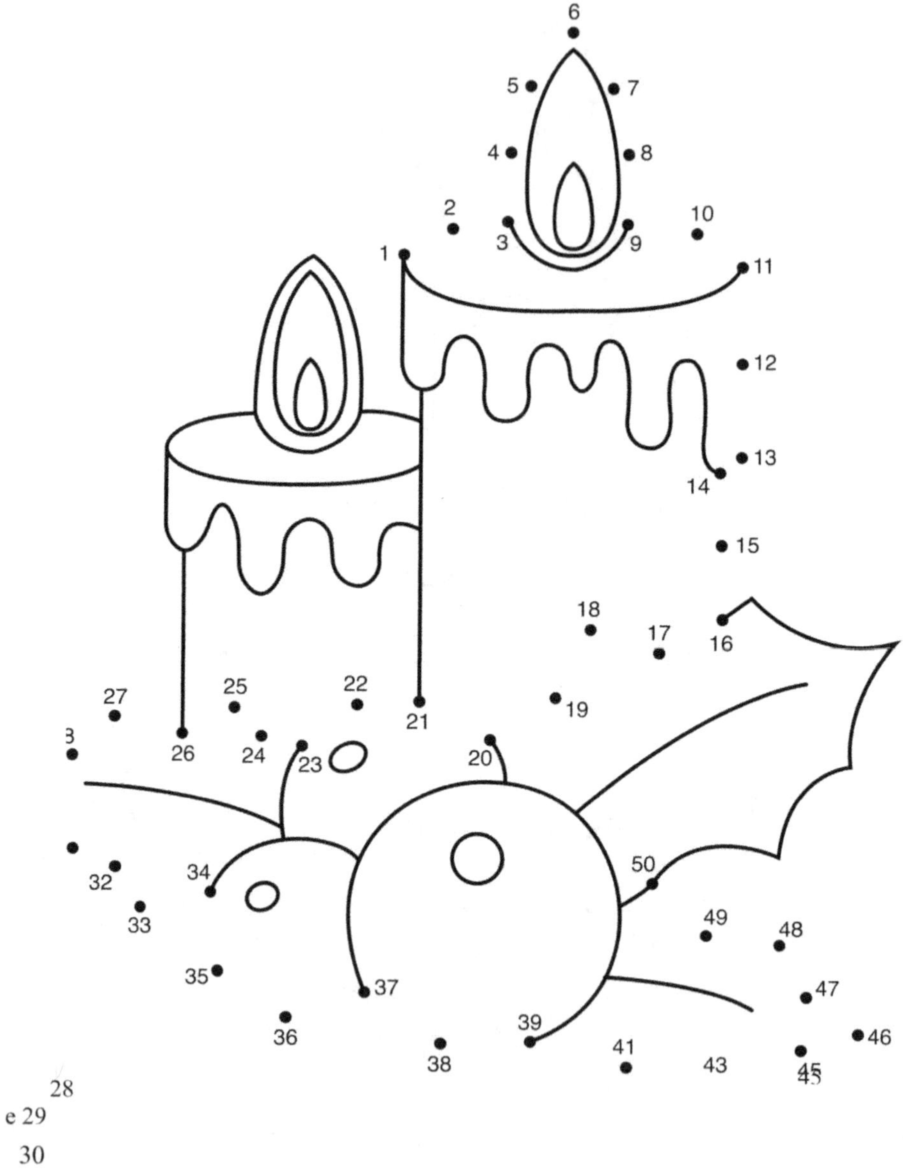

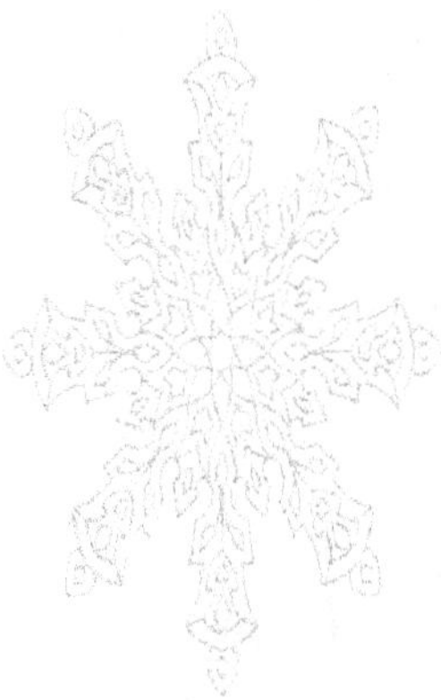

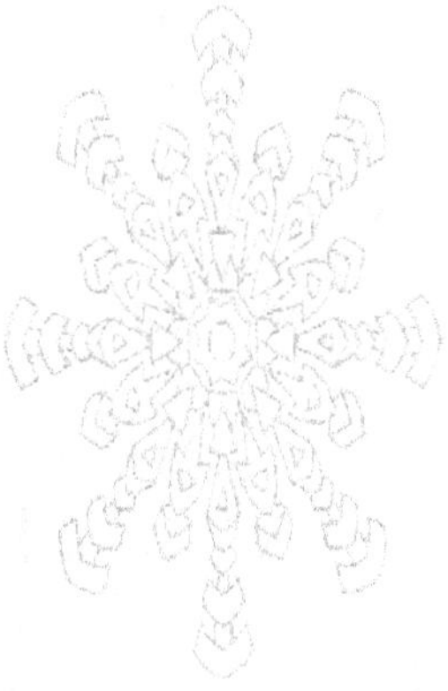

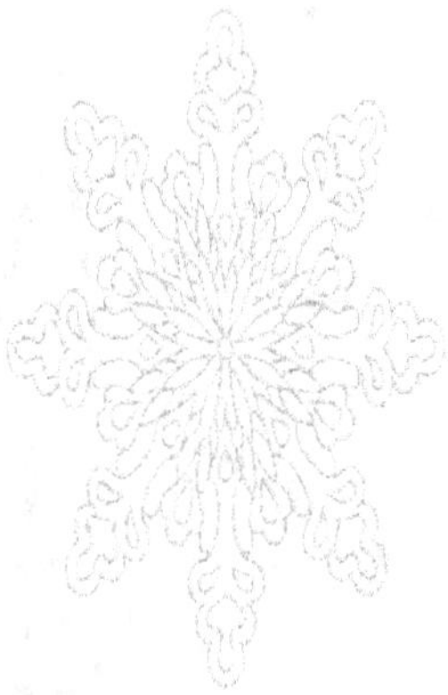

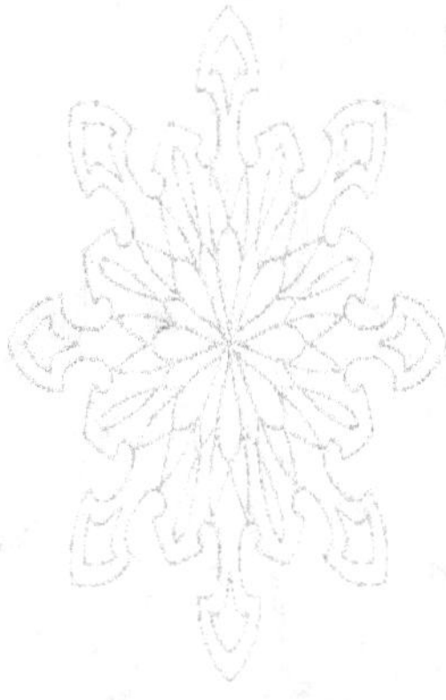
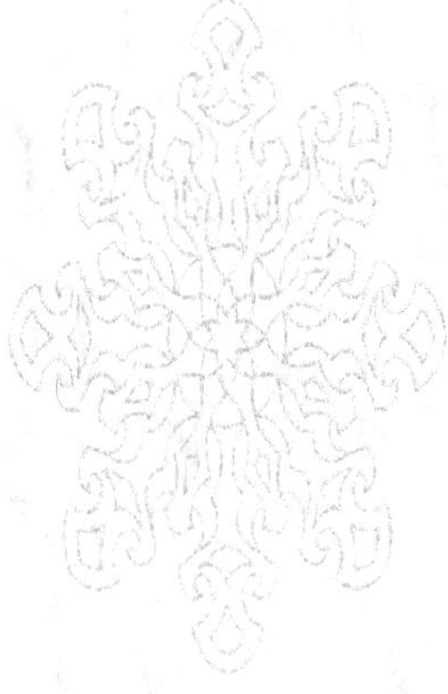

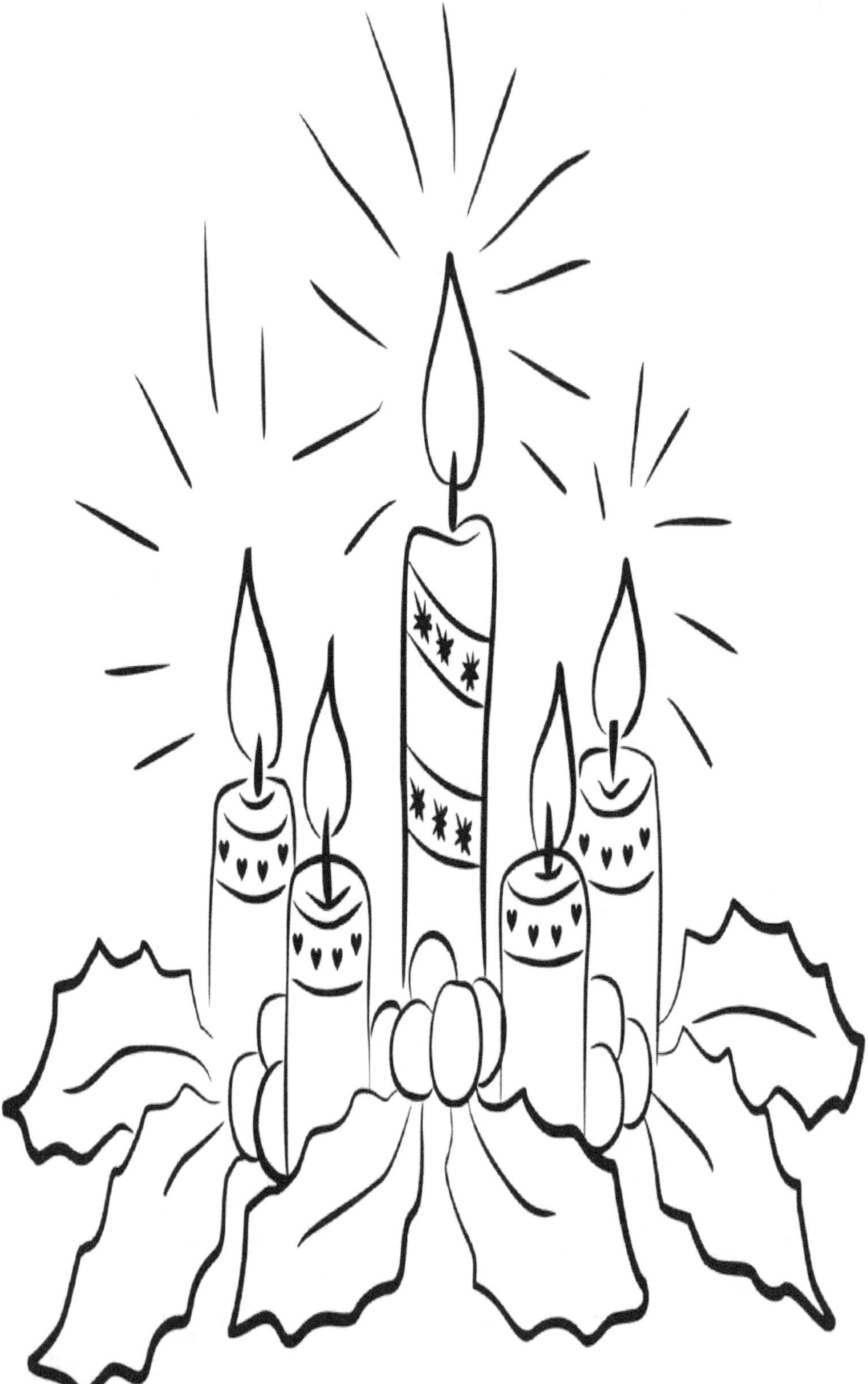

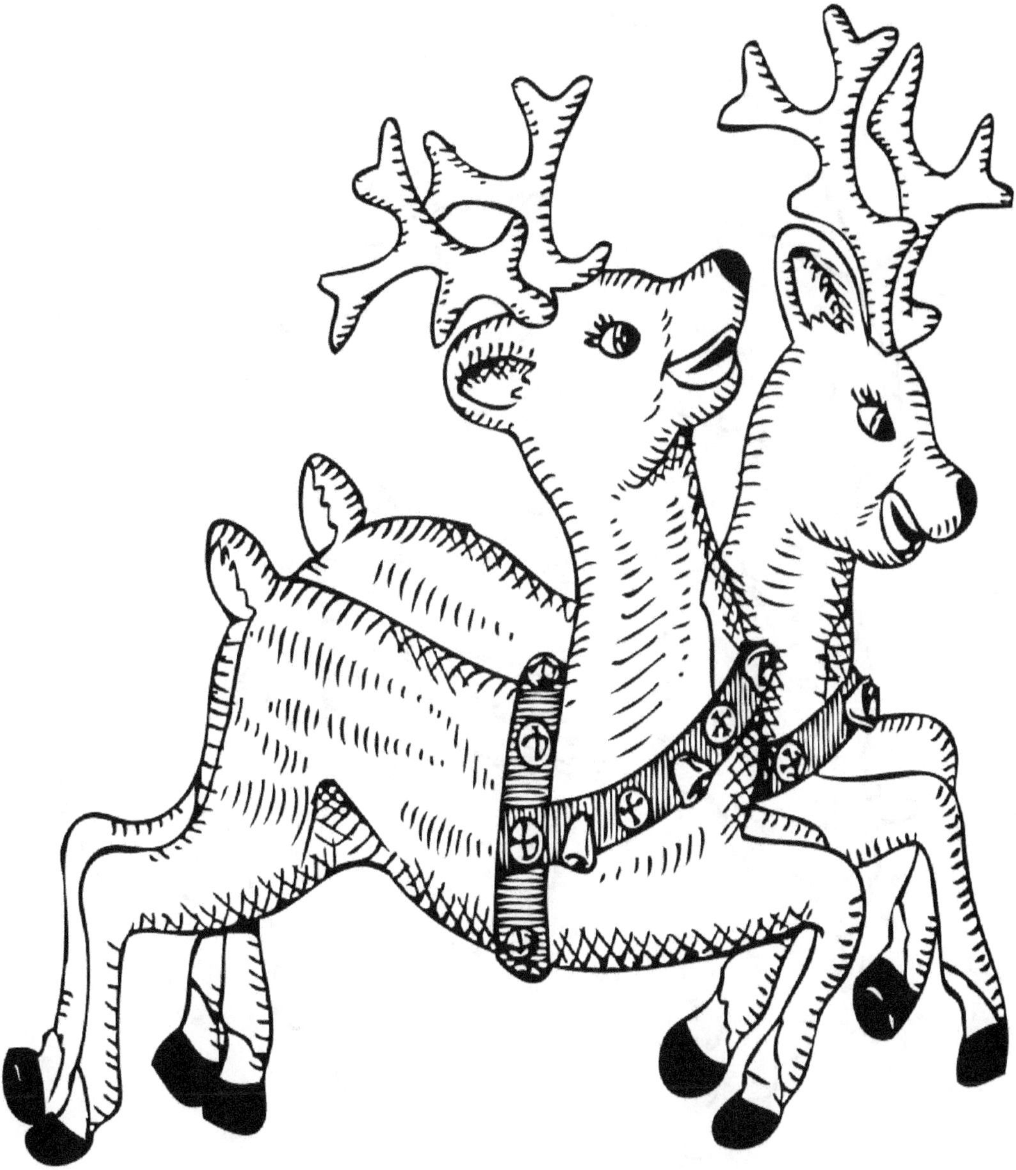

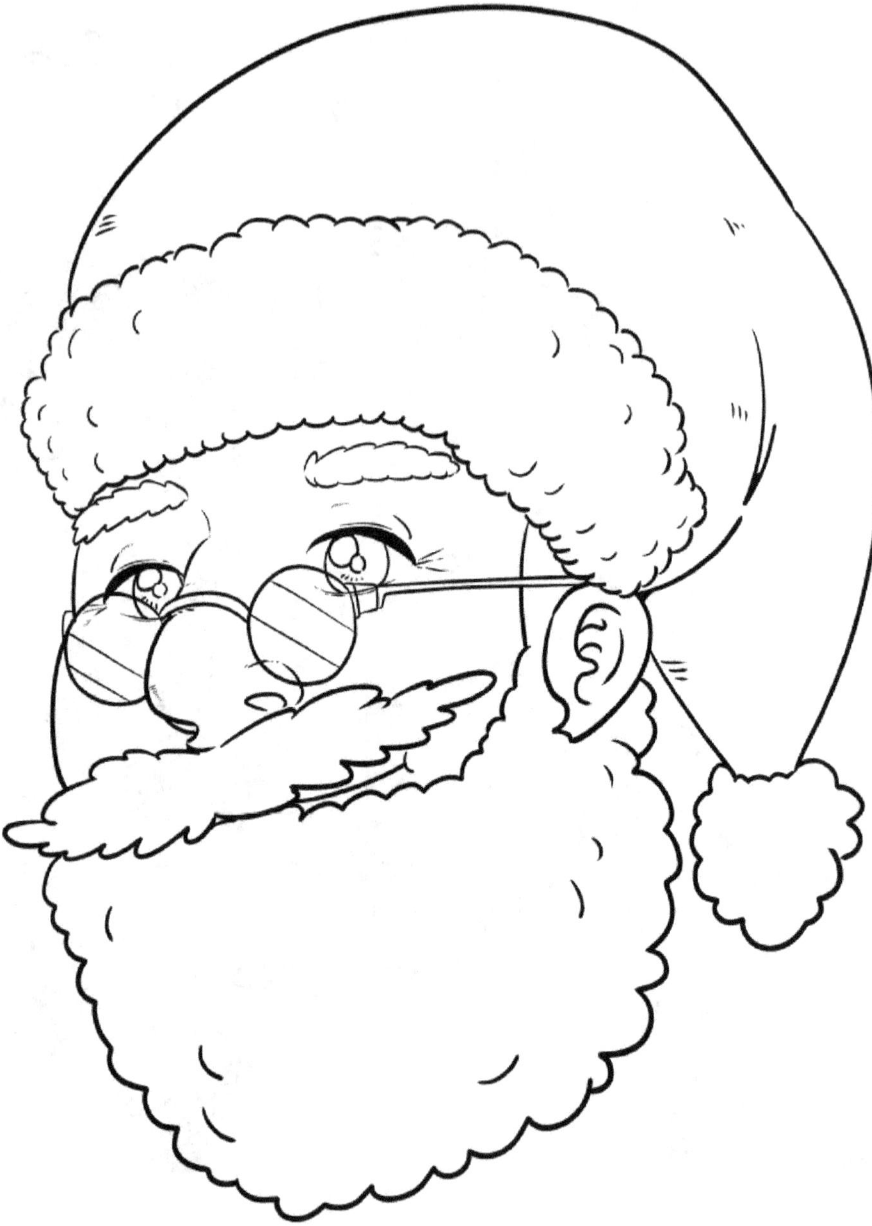

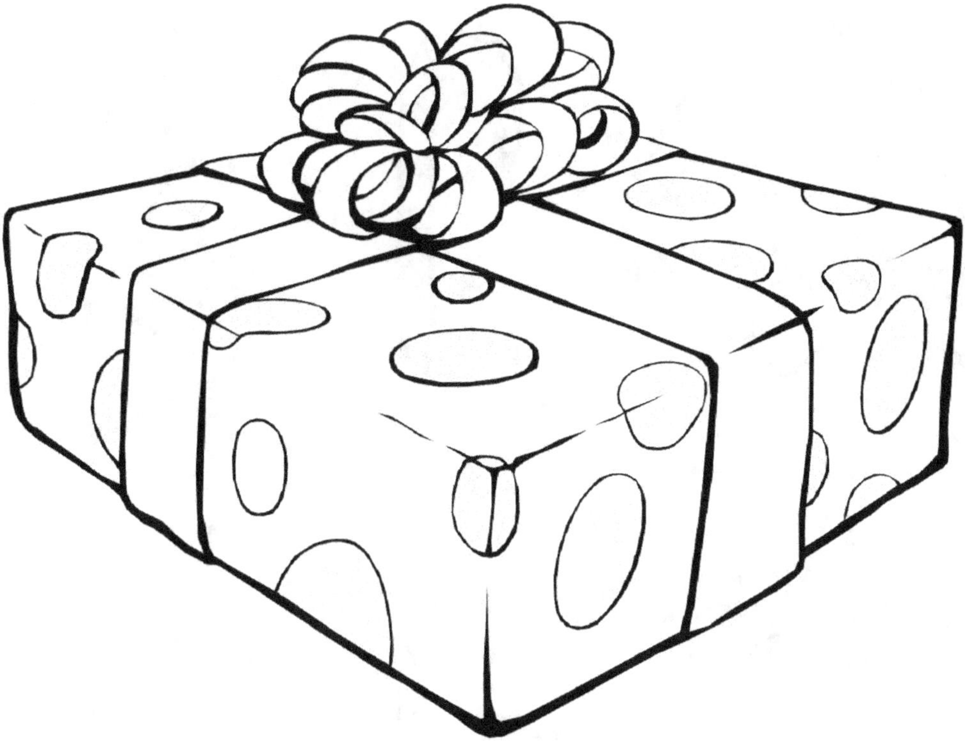

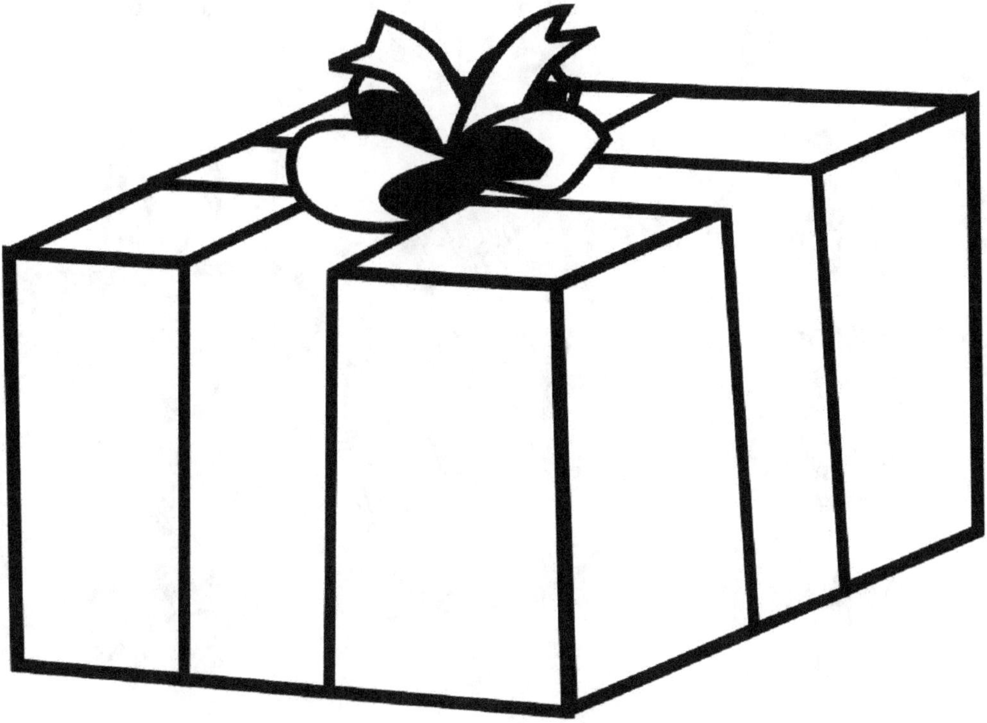

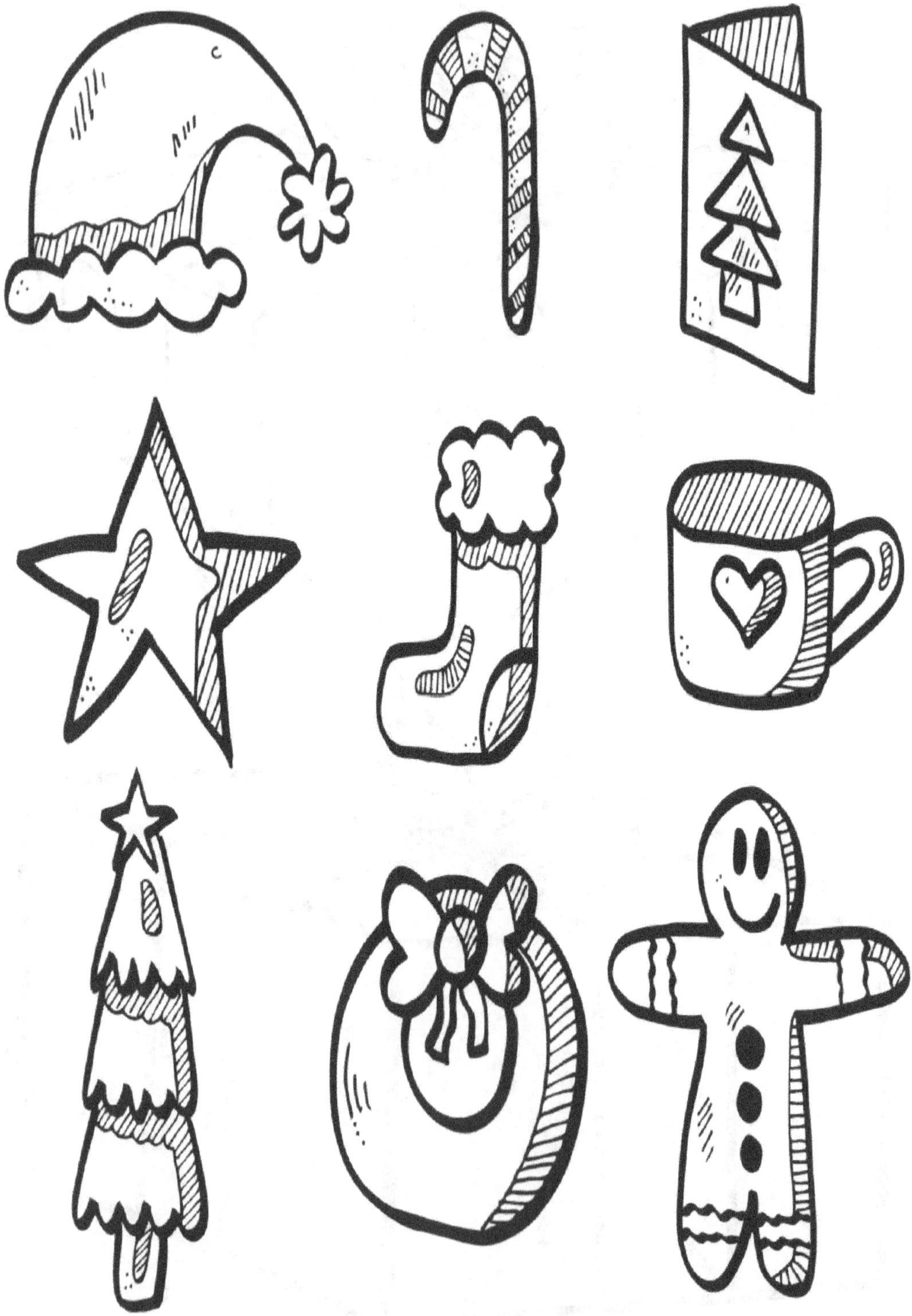

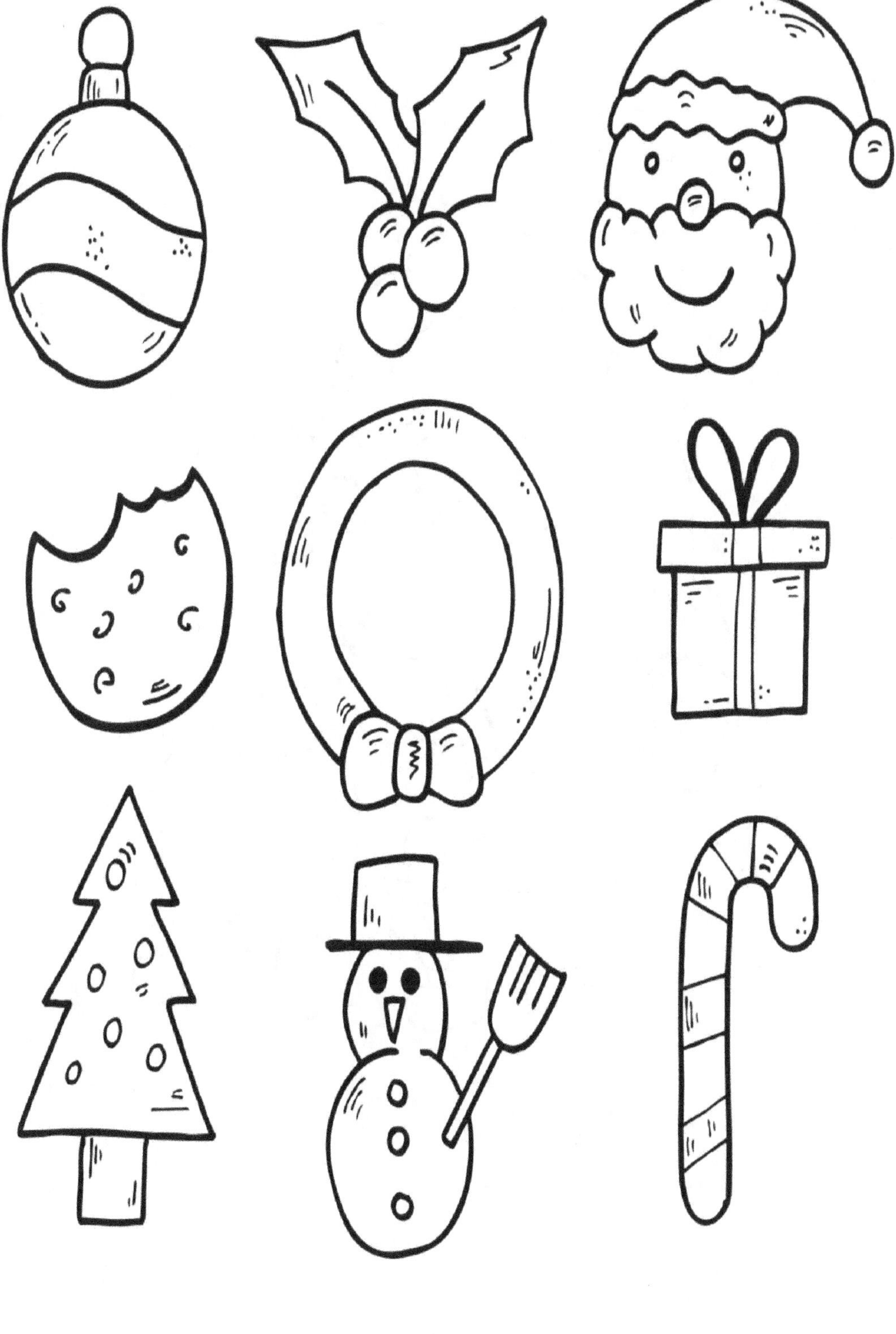

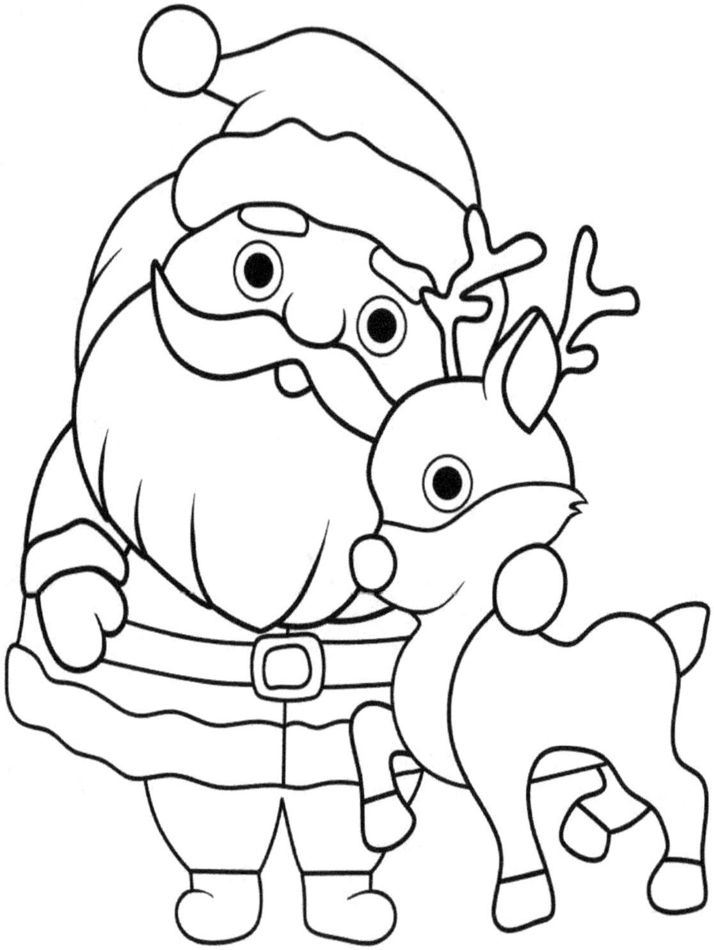

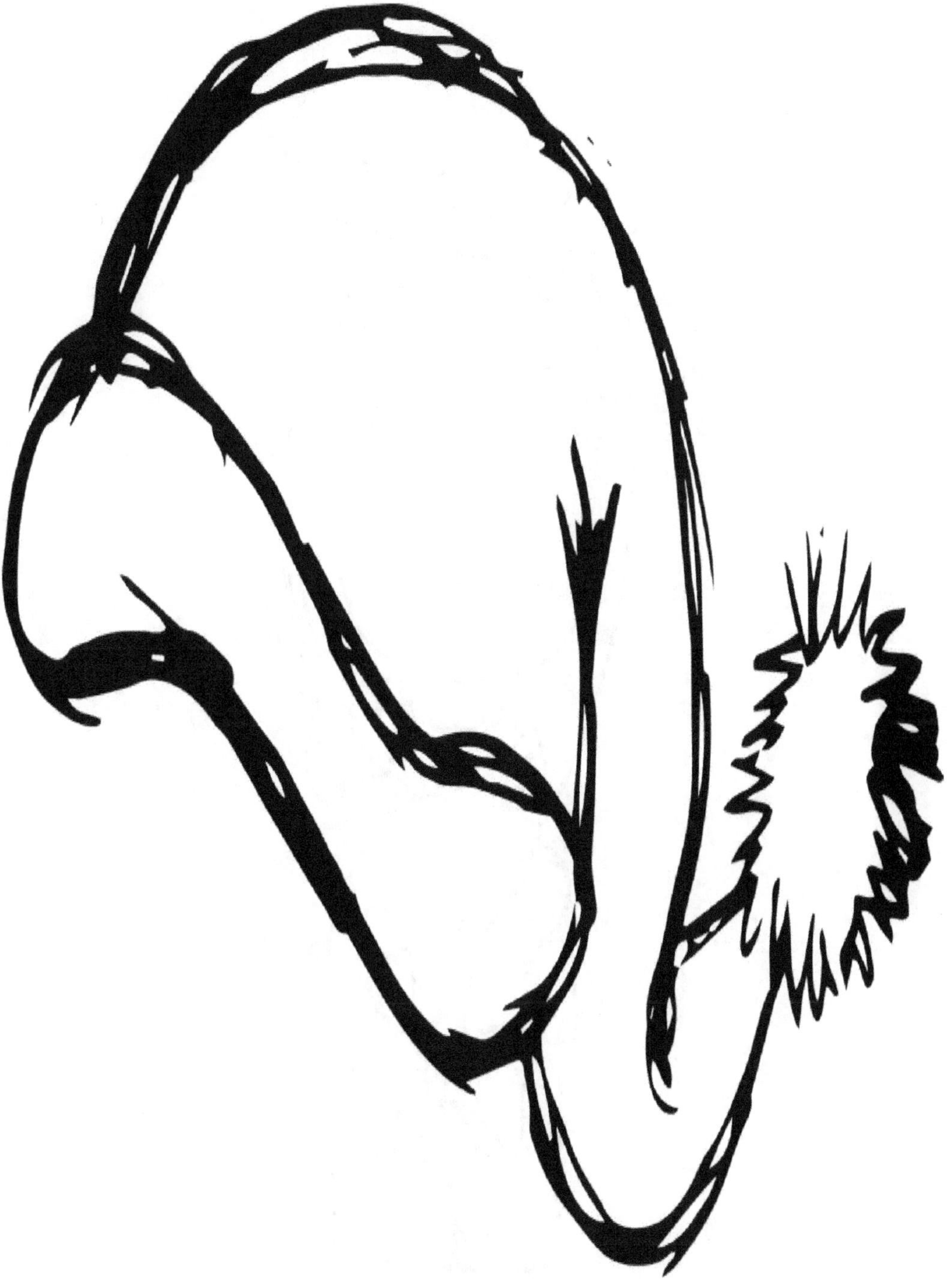

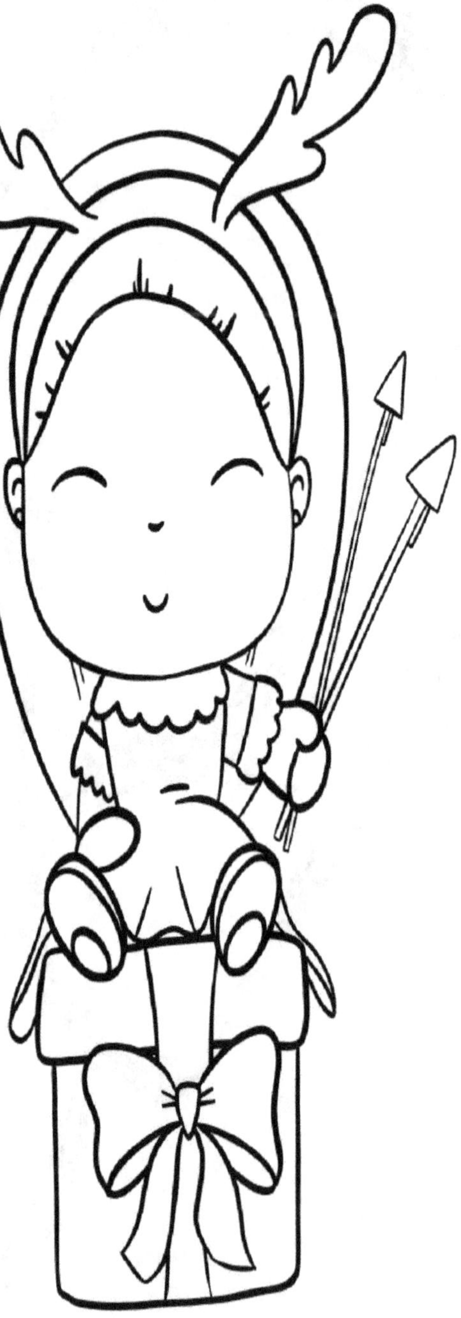

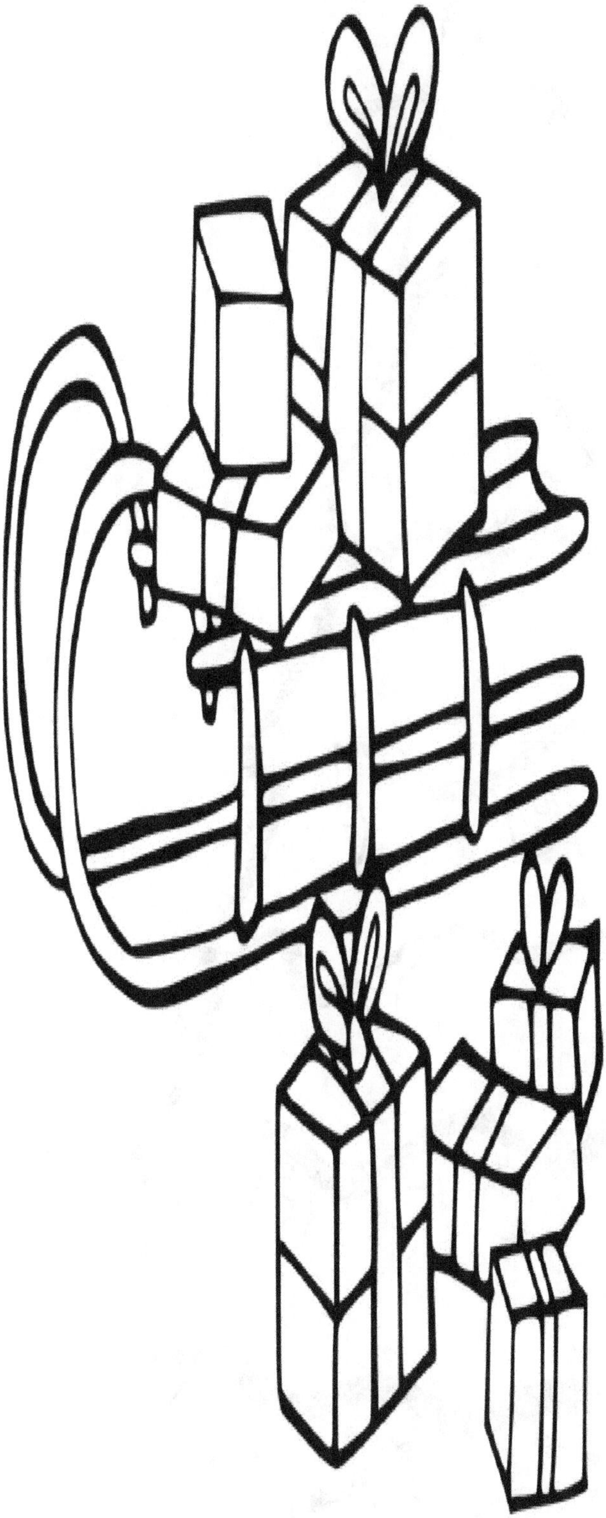

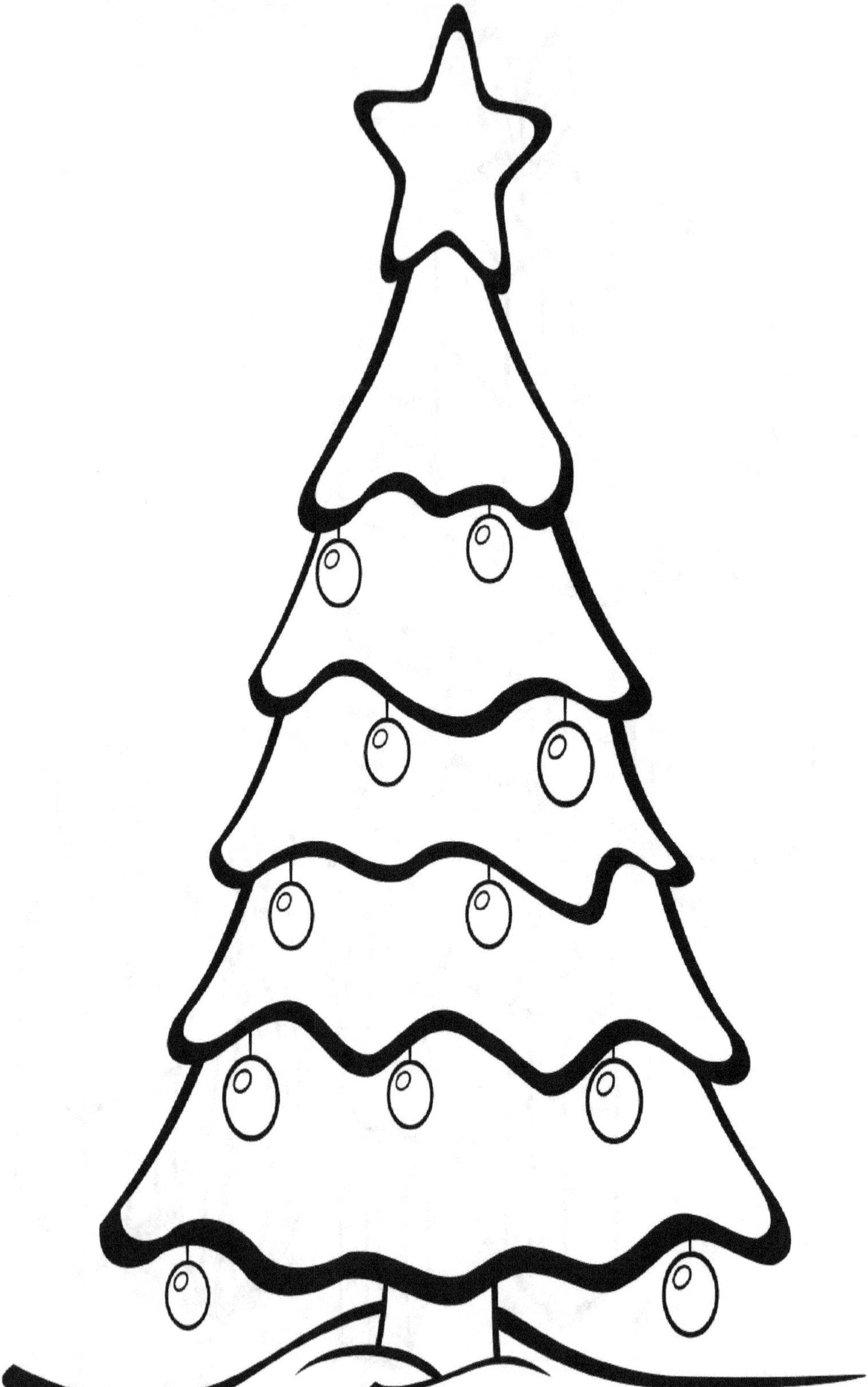

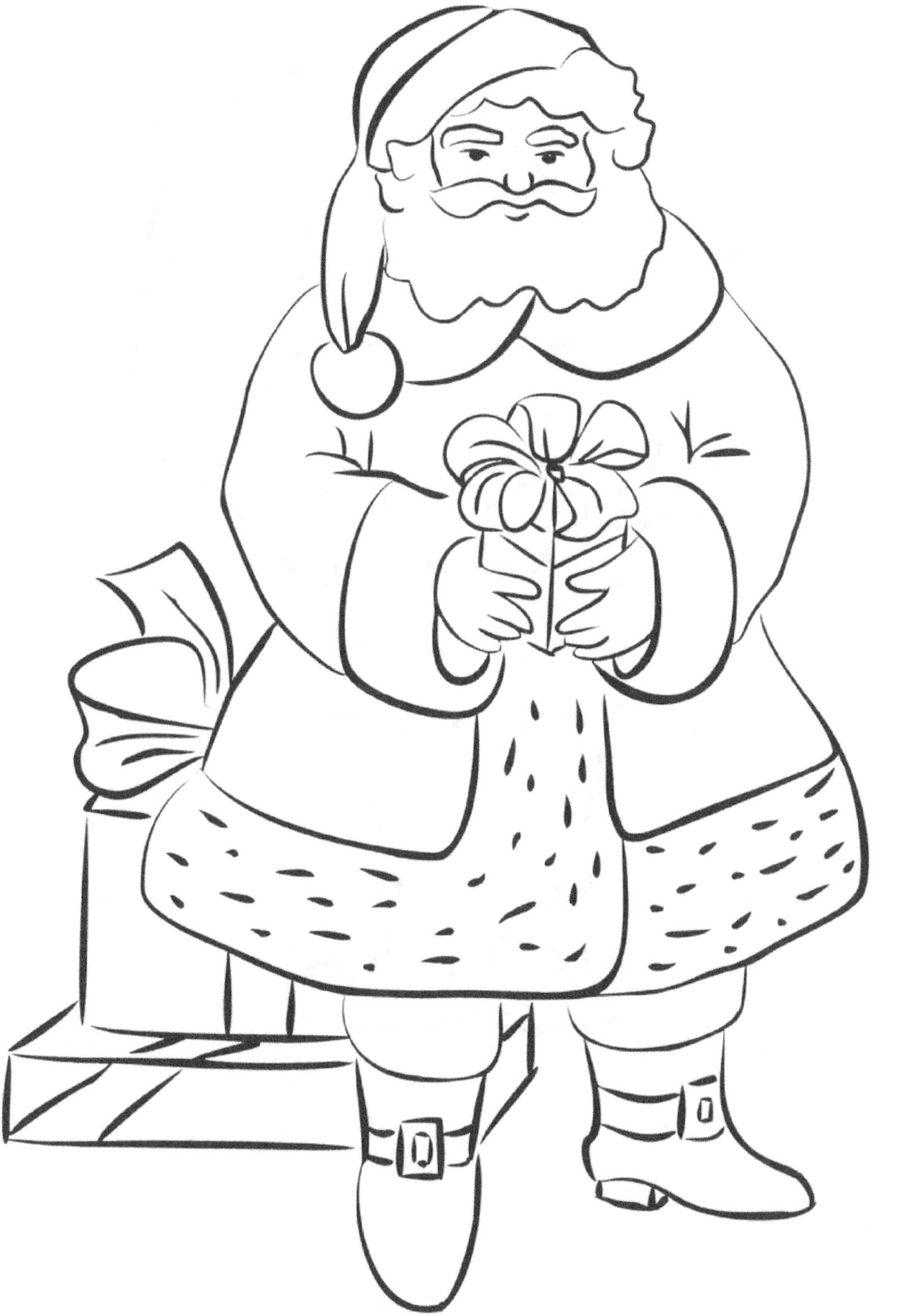

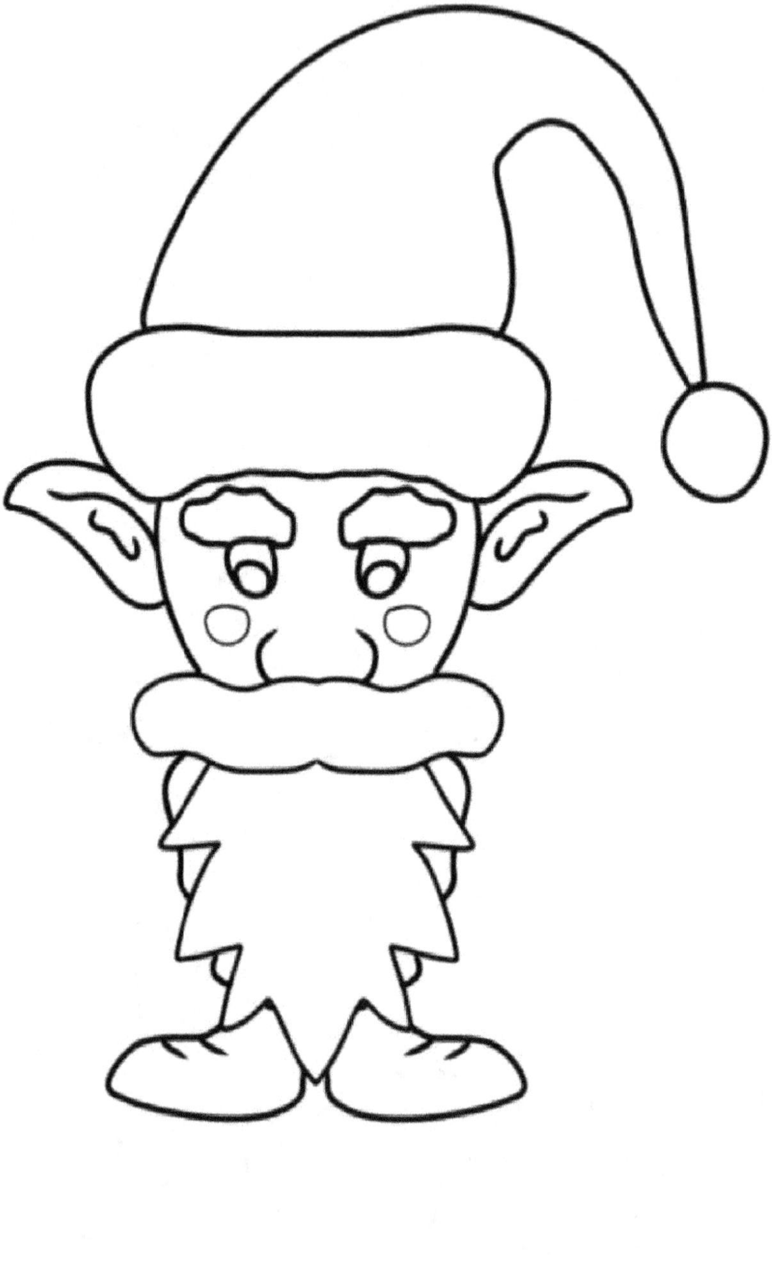

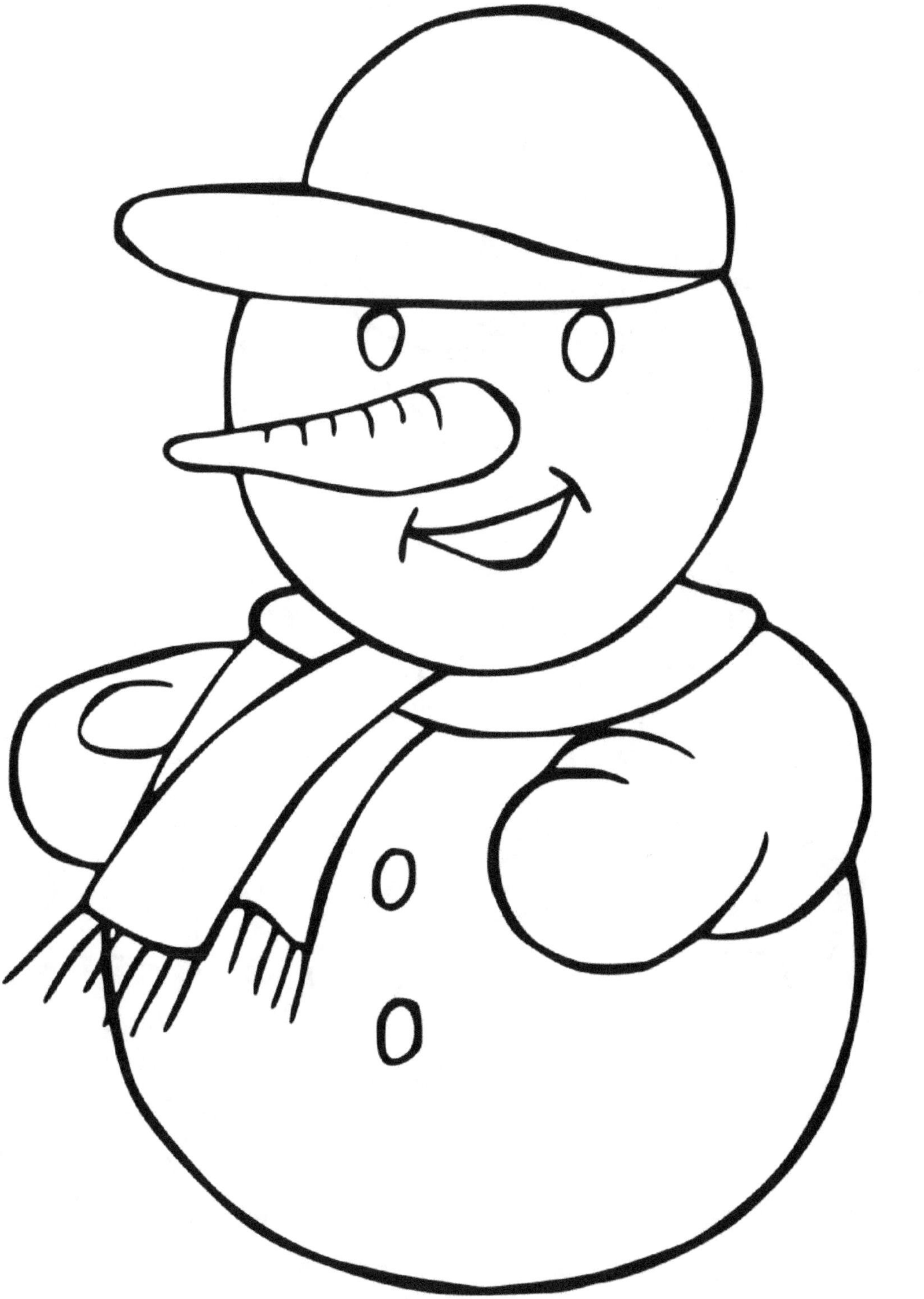

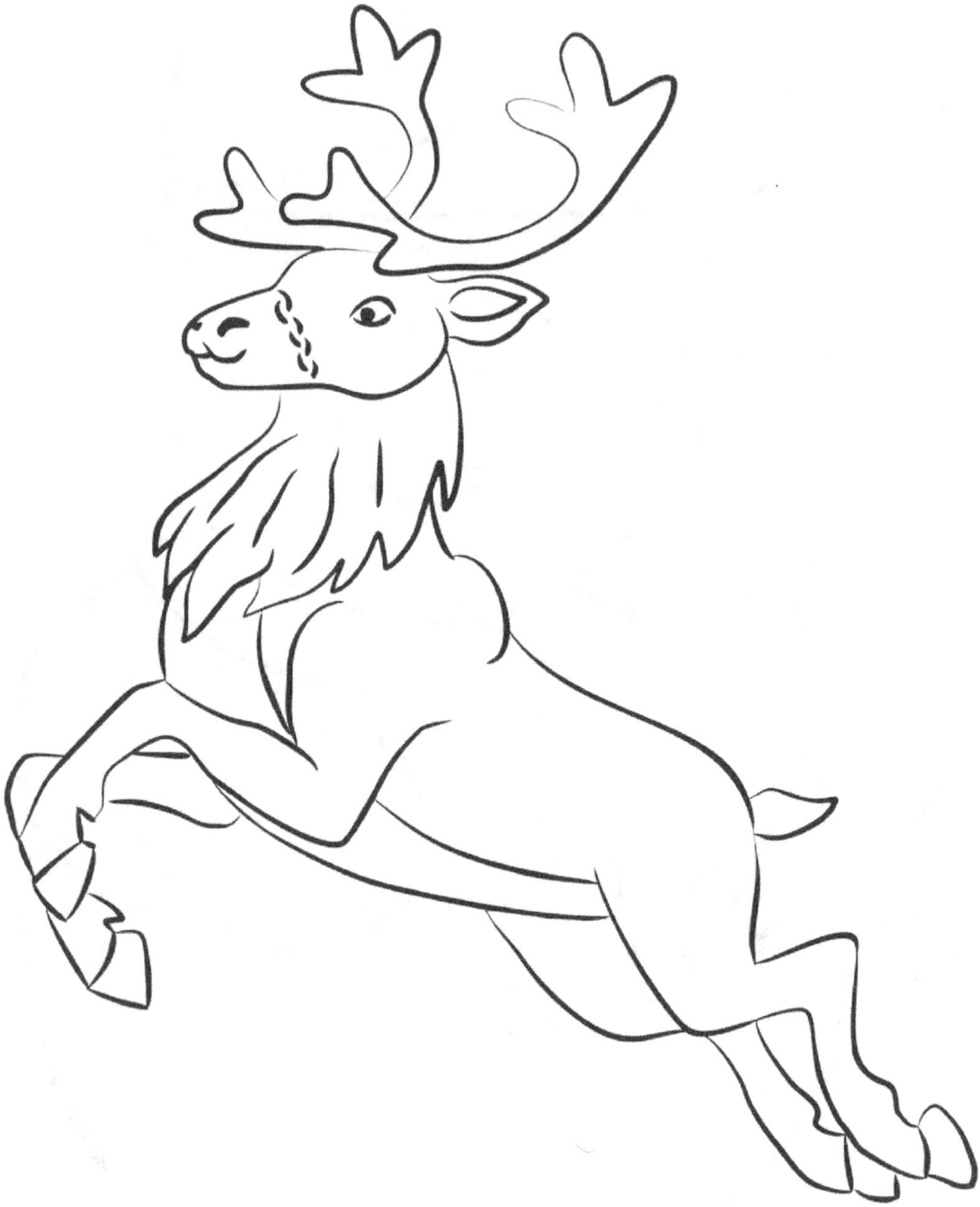

CHRISTMAS

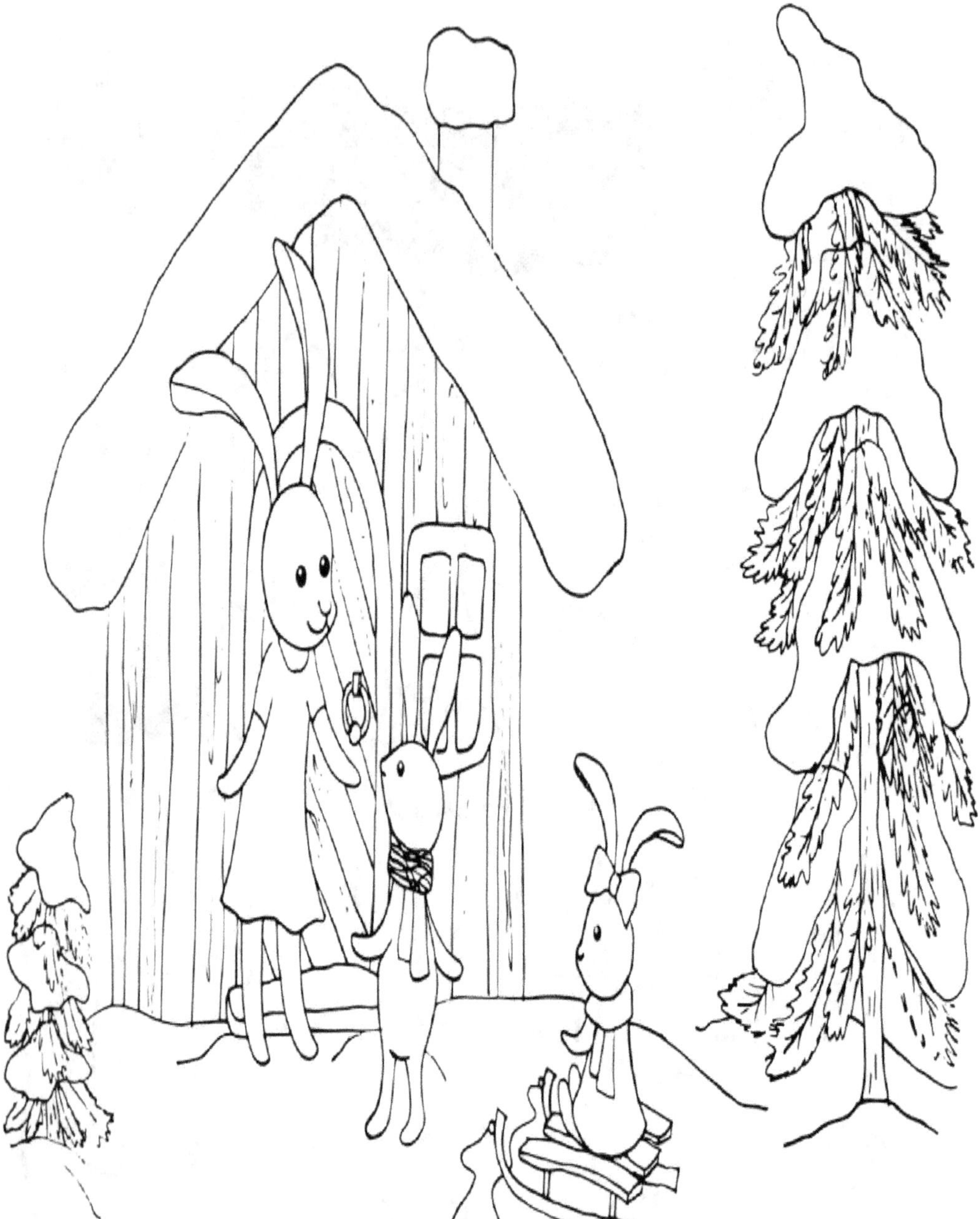

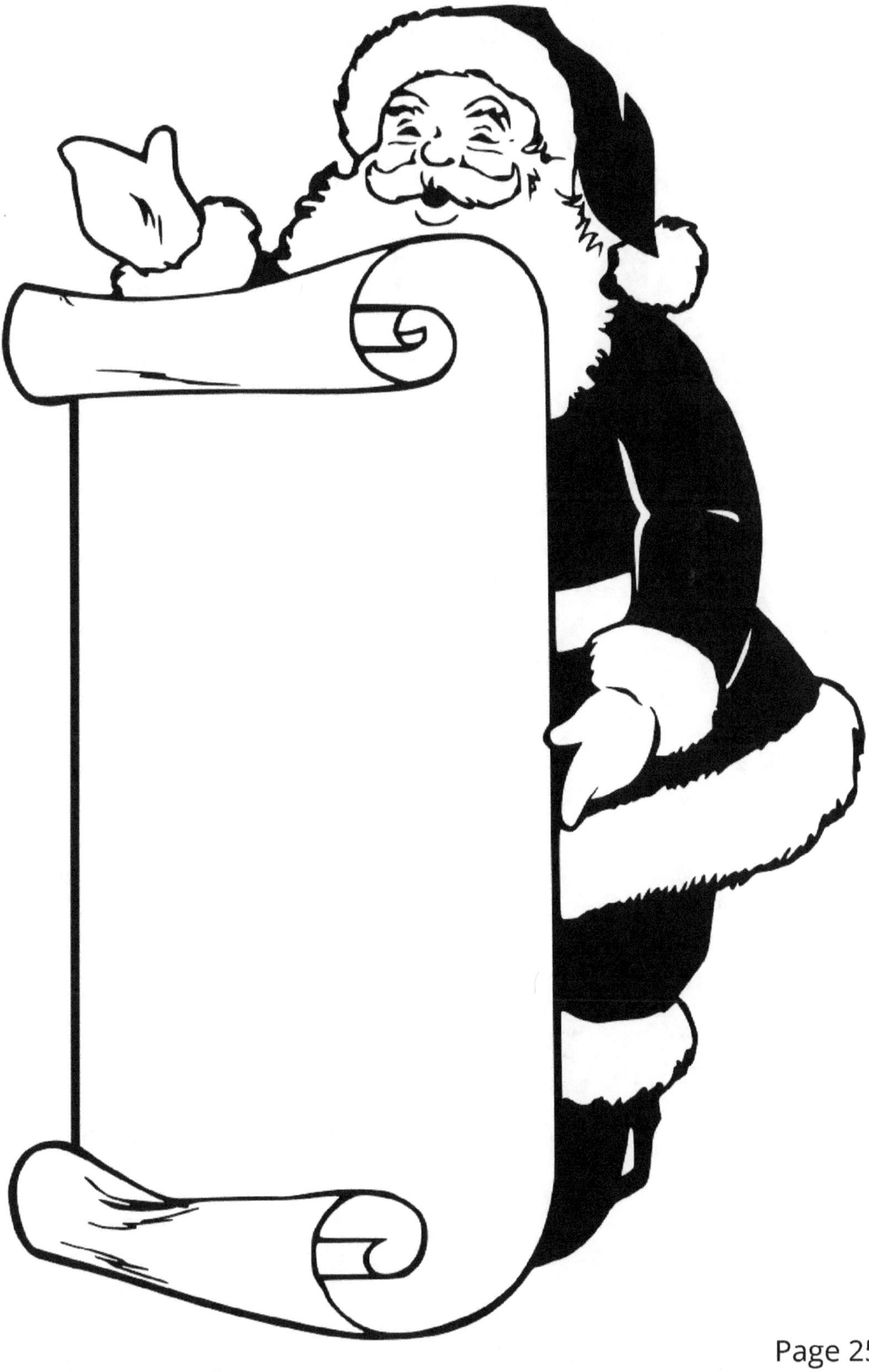

www.ingramcontent.com/pod-product-compliance
Lightning Source LLC
Chambersburg PA
CBHW050330220526
45465CB00005B/2210

* 9 7 9 8 3 6 3 1 1 8 1 4 2 *